The Nightingale

Story by
Hans Christian Andersen

Retold by **Jenny Giles**

Illustrated by **Xiangyi Mo
and Jingwen Wang**

PM Plus Chapter Books
Emerald

U.S. Edition © 2013 Houghton Mifflin Harcourt Publishing Company
125 High Street
Boston, MA 02110
www.hmhco.com

Text © 2003 Cengage Learning Australia Pty Limited
Illustrations © 2003 Cengage Learning Australia Pty Limited
Originally published in Australia by Cengage Learning Australia

18   1957   18
26517

Text: Retold by Jenny Giles
Illustrations: Xiangyi Mo and Jungwen Wang
Printed in China by 1010 Printing International Ltd

The Nightingale
ISBN 978 0 75 784118 7

Contents

Chapter One

The Palace by the Sea

Once upon a time, there was a king who lived in a magnificent palace high on a clifftop overlooking the sea. The palace was enormous. It had more than a hundred rooms, all filled with the finest furniture and the most precious ornaments.

The palace was surrounded by huge gardens, which were planted with all kinds of trees and flowers. The gardens stretched for miles, and no one quite knew where they ended. Not even the king had seen every part of them.

People came from all over the land to admire the splendid palace, and to gaze in wonder at the beautiful gardens.

Chapter Two

The Nightingale's Song

$\mathcal{E}$arly one morning, a nightingale flew into the palace gardens. She darted back and forth, admiring the colorful plants and flowers. After a while, she decided to make her home in a tall tree, which by chance was just outside the king's bedroom window.

The little brown nightingale perched on a branch and began to sing her beautiful song. The clear, pure notes sounded so lovely that all the gardeners stopped working, and all the servants stopped scurrying about inside the palace. They stood quite still and listened with delight.

The king, who had been sleeping, jumped out of bed and went to the window. The little bird saw him watching her, and so she sang her song again. The sound of it was lovelier than anything the king had ever heard. It brought tears of joy to his eyes.

"How can it be," he said to himself, "that such a plain little bird can sing such a wondrous song?"

The king had the little nightingale brought into the palace. He ordered that a special golden perch be made for her next to his throne, so that she could sing for him whenever he wished.

During the long summer days that followed, the nightingale's beautiful song could often be heard in the palace, and everyone worked happily as they listened to it.

Travelers from all over the world came to marvel at the wonderful melody. "The king's palace and gardens are indeed magnificent," they said, "but nothing is more beautiful than the song of the nightingale."

The king had everything in the world that he needed to make him happy.

Chapter Three

The Golden Bird

One day, a golden box arrived at the palace, with a note for the king. It was a present from an emperor who ruled over a distant land. The servants gathered around to listen as the king read the note aloud.

My good king,

I hear that you are fortunate enough to be surrounded by many fine things. You have a magnificent palace with wonderful gardens. You have more gold and silver and precious jewels than you will ever need. And you have a nightingale that sings the most beautiful song in the world for you.

But I have been told that your nightingale is a drab little bird — dull and brown, and not truly fit to live in a palace such as yours. So I have had another nightingale made for you. It is a wondrous bird, and it will provide you with many happy hours of music.

The king ordered one of his servants to open the box. Inside was a toy bird, just the same size as the nightingale! It was made of gold and covered with glittering jewels. Very carefully, the servant lifted the golden bird out of the box, and placed it on a table for all to see.

The king cried out in amazement. "What a magnificent bird!" he said. "Such brilliant jewels!" He took the bird in both hands and held it up to the light. As he did so, the jewels sparkled brightly, and everyone gasped.

Then the king turned a tiny key on the side of the golden bird, and placed it back on the table. The little golden wings began to move up and down, and the head moved from side to side. The golden beak opened, and sweet notes like the tinkling of a bell floated through the palace.

The mechanical bird could sing the same song as the real nightingale!

The king was overjoyed. "I have two nightingales now!" he cried. "I will have them sing a duet for me. What a wonderful sound that will be!"

And so it was. The birds sang in chorus, and everyone who heard their song was enchanted by the melody. And how they admired the golden bird, with its wings covered in sparkling jewels!

"You have been given a most remarkable gift," they told the king. "You are indeed fortunate to own such a treasure!"

Chapter Four

The Nightingale Flies Away

As the days passed, the nightingale grew tired of waiting for the mechanical bird to be wound up. She grew tired of singing the same melody again and again, and tired of the way the visitors admired the golden bird and its brilliant jewels.

One evening, the nightingale flew out
through the palace window. No one saw
her go. The king was busy winding up his
golden bird for the people who had waited
for hours outside the palace gates. He did
not miss the little brown bird at all.

The nightingale flew to the very edge of the king's gardens. She found a tree overlooking the sea, and there she sang her song to the fishermen below, and to the travelers who sailed by in boats.

19

Chapter Five

The Golden Bird Sings Its Last Song

As the years went by, the king grew old and frail. The golden bird still sang its song, but quite slowly now, and it needed to be wound more often. Most of the time, the king stayed in his room, listening to the melody over and over again.

But the golden bird was beginning to wear out.

One day, with a final click and a tired whir, it stopped altogether. The king ordered his servants to mend it, but nothing could be done. The king was bitterly disappointed. His precious bird would never sing again.

Brokenhearted, the king lay down on his bed. There he stayed, day after day, week after week, hardly moving at all.

Word spread throughout the land that the king was very ill, and people gathered outside the castle, waiting for news of him. There was a feeling of sadness in the crowd, for he had been a good and kind king, and no one wanted him to die.

Chapter Six

The Nightingale Returns

Then one day, the nightingale flew over the castle and noticed the crowd of people gathered below. She found her way to her favorite tree outside the king's bedroom window. As she perched on a branch, she looked in through the window and saw the king lying pale and still.

The little bird felt sorry for him and wanted nothing more than to make him happy again.

And so the nightingale's beautiful song was heard in the palace gardens once again. The clear, pure notes floated into the room where the king was lying.

When the king heard the lovely melody, he thought that he was dreaming. But when he opened his eyes, he saw the nightingale singing to him from her branch in the tree. For the first time in many months, he smiled. Tears of happiness rolled down his cheeks.

As the song ended, the king left his bed and walked slowly to the window. "Little bird," he said, "I have treated you badly. Yet you came to me when I needed you most. You and your beautiful song mean more to me than all the gold and jewels in the world."

When she heard these words, the little nightingale was filled with great joy.

And as she sang her sweet melody over and over again, the crowd below rejoiced to see their beloved king standing at the palace window. They knew that with the return of the nightingale, all would be well in the kingdom once more.

All About...
Hans Christian Andersen

Hans Christian Andersen was born in Denmark, in 1805. His family was very poor, and he didn't have a good education, but he always loved to tell stories. As he grew older, he wrote many novels and poems for adults, but his stories for children were more successful.

Most of Hans's stories were based on his own life. *The Nightingale* was written about an opera singer named Jenny Lind. Jenny was known as the "Swedish Nightingale," because she had a beautiful voice. Hans loved her, but she did not love him in return.

By the time of his death in 1875, Hans Christian Andersen had become one of the most famous writers in the world. His stories, which include *The Ugly Duckling*, *The Little Mermaid*, *The Emperor's New Clothes*, and *The Little Match Girl*, were loved by children and adults alike. They continue to delight people all over the world.